THE **L** GROUP
Leadership at every level.

theLgroup.com

Praise for
The 5 Coaching Habits of Excellent Leaders

"*The 5 Coaching Habits* describes the daily challenge of coaching in simple terms and brings it to life with engaging examples. The authors' encouraging style and practical tools empower leaders to take positive action for their teams."

Daniel Jones
CEO, Encore Wire

"The authors cracked the coaching code! They simplified the art of coaching into five easily communicated and applied steps. Thank you, Lee, for being an outstanding, RELIABLE leader and coach!"

Jerry Crawford
CEO, Jani-King International, Inc.

"Lee Colan and Julie Davis-Colan provide a timely and relevant book every leader and aspiring leader should read. As the authors so aptly point out, 'the best way to coach reliability is to be personally reliable.' A good first step would be to read this book."

Joel T. Allison
former CEO, Baylor Scott & White Health

"The authors know it's not about complex competencies or innate skills – it's about the simple and clear things we DO every day. No scripts or flow charts to remember – just powerful behaviors paired with proven tools to boost team performance."

Dean Carter
Chief Administrative Officer, Patagonia

"After almost 20 years of being coached by Lee on many of these principles, I am thankful that he has put them in writing. As a coaches' coach, Lee delivers great and practical insights to help every leader be a better coach. Consistent with previous books, Lee and Juie are to the point and deliver practical tools that leaders can apply immediately."

Barry E. Davis
CEO, EnLink Midstream

"Lee Colan really, really gets it. He has a unique skill of converting complex leadership concepts into an easy-to-understand, practical approach. He has done it again in *The 5 Coaching Habits*. His blend of experience and know-how is hard to find. If you want engaged, or better yet, inspired leaders – he is the man!"

Dave Loeser
Sr. Vice President, Worldwide Human Resources, Unisys

"We all know great leaders need to be good coaches, but this book very succinctly clarifies and simplifies the coaching habits of excellent leaders. The authors keep it short and sweet in delivering actionable tools to help leaders elevate their coaching game."

Andrew Levi
CEO, Blue Calypso

"*The 5 Coaching Habits of Excellent Leaders* is a handy field guide for every leader. The authors deliver simple but powerful tools that you can put to work with your team right away. It is a quick-read, high-impact resource!"

Terry Looper
CEO, Texon

"Ever since I read Lee and Julie's book, *Sticking to It: The Art of Adherence*, I have been a fan. Their ability to reduce the complexity of leadership to a simple, concise set of habits and principles sets them apart. Even more importantly, by reading this short book, a good leader can become an excellent leader by focusing on their five coaching habits."

Dennis McCuistion
Television host and Executive Director
The Institute for Excellence in Corporate Governance
The University of Texas at Dallas

"Lee and Julie articulate that great leaders choose to meet the needs of their team over any personal discomforts. This choice is made through first knowing yourself and then having clarity in establishing priorities in business and life. I highly recommend this leadership journey for anyone who wants to improve themselves and their team."

Craig Dunaway
President, Penn Station East Coast Subs

"Three cheers to Lee and Julie. They've done it again! The Colans are reliably reliable! When they speak, I listen."

Denis G. Simon
Senior Executive Vice President,
Challenger, Gray & Christmas, Inc.

"The authors' approach and tools for how excellent leaders build reliable teams is paramount to delivering excellent business results."

Tom Pajonas,
COO, Flowserve

"Lee has written another insightful coaching book that will be an excellent resource for new or seasoned business leaders. I've utilized Lee's talents and tools over the years. Whether coaching new or experienced leaders, I've found Lee's coaching style and methods to be extremely effective. Well done!"

Chuck Jerasa
Group President, Gibraltar Industries

"The 5 Coaching Habits of Excellent Leaders is just that … EXCELLENT! What a fantastic reminder of the fundamental value of reliability, personally, and as a coach to your team. This is clearly the most straightforward and immediately useable treatment of this topic available today."

Scott Florence
Vice President, Sales, AdvoCare Int'l

"Reliability is, indeed, the most fundamental element of differentiation. The authors have captured this essential ingredient and incorporated the steps for 'reliability' in *The 5 Coaching Habits*. The book itself has achieved differentiation through 'reliability'... advice you can count on!"

Jim Keyes
former CEO, 7-Eleven and Blockbuster

"The 5 Coaching Habits is filled with powerful insights and practical tips. It's a must-have guide for leaders at all levels. Kudos to Lee and Julie for providing yet another powerful tool for the leader's tool box!"

Sharon Goldstein
Campus Operating Officer, Berkeley College Online

Other Books by the Authors:

- *Sticking to It: The Art of Adherence*

- *Passionate Performance: Engaging Minds and Hearts to Conquer the Competition*

- *Orchestrating Attitude: Getting the Best from Yourself and Others*

- *107 Ways to Stick to It*

- *7 Moments … That Define Excellent Leaders*

- *Leadership Matters: Daily Insights to Inspire Extraordinary Results*

- *Power Exchange: Boosting Accountability and Performance in Today's Workforce*

- *Inspire! Connecting with Students to Make a Difference*

- *The Nature of Excellence*

- *Winners Always Quit: Seven Pretty Good Habits You Can Swap for Really Great Results*

The 5 Coaching Habits of Excellent Leaders

of

How to Create  for Your Team

FROM THE BEST-SELLING AUTHORS OF
STICKING TO IT: THE ART OF ADHERENCE

Lee J. Colan, Ph.D.
Julie Davis-Colan

The 5
Coaching Habits
of Excellent Leaders

How to Create the Reliability Advantage for Your Team

CornerStone Leadership Institute
P.O. Box 764087
Dallas, TX 75376
888.789.5323

Printed in the United States of America
ISBN: 978-0-9961469-4-4

Credits

Copy Editor	Steve Williford, Memphis, TN
Proofreaders	Kathleen Green, Positively Proofed, Plano, TX
	info@PositivelyProofed.com
	Jami Wilmarth, Amarillo, TX
Design, art direction & production	Melissa Farr, Back Porch Creative, Frisco, TX
	info@BackPorchCreative.com

Table of Contents

Introduction

————

Reliability is a team sport, and like any team sport, it requires a good coach.

Consider this scenario: It's early February. Jack Samuels, a sales director for a large logistics company, just landed back in Chicago and is now driving to his suburban home from the airport. He pulled off a successful pitch to a new customer in Dallas earlier that day, his final ticket to punch before the promised promotion to a VP role. The thrill of victory is running through his veins as he considers not only the pitch but also how he arrived on time against all odds. As he sits in standstill traffic with worsening road conditions from ice, Jack reflects on his team. Team members pulled off a big win by reliably performing their roles despite a series of obstacles, and it yielded the desired result for all involved.

Jack's mind drifts to all the others he had to rely on today to make the pitch possible. He realizes that he couldn't have even made it to the meeting in Dallas without a series of people from the airline team doing their jobs reliably: the curbside attendant quickly checking him in and tagging the big box of presentation boards to beat the 30-minute deadline, the gate agent persistently paging his name to ensure he was not left behind, the flight attendants politely hustling passengers into their seats, the de-icers timing their process just right, the pilots doing their dozens of checks to ensure all were safe, the baggage guys who loaded and unloaded his big box of materials, and the maintenance and food service teams who are invisible to Jack but, no doubt, played a part.

Then Jack's appreciation deepens as he thinks of their monumental task of delivering reliable performance many, many times each day through hundreds of teams and thousands of team members. He is motivated to boost his personal reliability each day so that he can inspire more reliable performance from his team, an even bigger team with his pending promotion.

You might have experienced a similar scenario at some point where, like Jack, you could see and appreciate the connection between personal and team reliability and its profound impact on the customer. We all inherently value reliability. It goes way beyond our air travel needs. Every day we value:

- Reliable cars that save time and money on repairs.

- Reliable mail that gets delivered on time.

- Reliable investments that deliver expected returns.

- Reliable cell phone service to stay connected.

- Reliable vendors who show up on time.

- Reliable restaurants that serve quality food and give good service.

- Reliable friends and colleagues who do what they say.

Each of these outcomes we value is achieved by a team even though, in some cases, an individual is delivering the service. Of course we all know the results of dealing with unreliable people and teams. They cost us more time and money, two things we all would like more of. Further, unreliability costs us more frustration and more stress, two things we would all like less of.

We have coached, trained and equipped more than 100,000 leaders to elevate their leadership since 1999. It has been evident that being an excellent coach is central to being an excellent leader. So, it's no surprise that much of our time is spent helping clients become better coaches, and ultimately better leaders.

The reliability value chain links leaders and profits:

Reliable leaders coach to
inspire reliable teams that
create reliable services and products that
generate reliable business results that
produce reliable growth and profits.

In today's environment of high-velocity change, technology, product innovation and unique distribution are only fleeting advantages. In fact, the only *sustainable* competitive advantage is an organization's talent and how reliably it performs. The goal of this book is to equip you to coach your team to perform more reliably and help your business deliver more reliable service, products and profits.

The Reliability Advantage has a multiplier effect … and it's you! Your personal reliability has a disproportionate impact on your team's reliability. You must be personally reliable before you can effectively coach your team to generate reliable results. So, in the first part of the book we will describe keys to build your personal reliability before we address the five coaching habits of excellent leaders.

A good coach can change a game.
A great coach can change a life.

– JOHN WOODEN,
former UCLA basketball coach
and 10-time champion

Personal
RELIABILITY

---- ★ ----

*Reliable people consider their commitments
as personal promises to others.*

---- ★ ----

A business that delivers reliable results is the sum of reliable teams, and reliable teams are the sum of reliable individuals. So, building reliable business results really starts with a leader coaching each team member to deliver reliable individual results.

Personal reliability is a cornerstone of leadership. Ken May began working at FedEx while he was in college. He started at the bottom sorting packages. He gradually worked his way up, becoming the Senior Vice President of North American Operations. He then became CEO of FedEx Kinko's and is currently CEO of Topgolf. When asked about his career climb, May is quick to say, "I just work hard at whatever I do. I don't complain. I don't blame. I just work hard. I'm grateful for my job, my organization and my customers. I try to never promise what I can't deliver."

May knows that he can't expect anything from his employees that he isn't willing to model. His employees know they have a boss, a friend and an example in May. He, in turn, has a loyal workforce. As May has been heard to say, "Personal reliability at the top is the beginning of a successful organization, a dedicated workforce and loyal customers."[1]

Leadership is an inside job. It starts inside with your personal leadership traits, such as integrity, trust, competence, authenticity – all of which are aspects of personal reliability. In fact, our company logo is a group of three stacked L's representing the three levels of leadership: personal, team and organizational. You cannot expect your team to be reliable (or any other trait for that matter) if *you* are not being reliable. Since reliability, like leadership, is built from the inside out, the most important question a leader should ask is, "*How reliable am I?*"

Reliability is like rain – everyone knows they need it, but no one wants to get wet. It's easy to talk about how "they" need to be more reliable, but it can be uncomfortable when we look in the mirror. When was the last time you heard someone say, "I really need to be more reliable"? We want to collect reliable people in our lives and on our teams. We do not want to deal with those who are unreliable. Think about it. Reliable people get and keep friends more easily, forge deeper relationships, receive the best opportunities, are granted more autonomy at work, have more self-confidence, live with integrity and carry a clear conscience. Before we address the five coaching habits of excellent leaders that inspire reliable results, let's focus on the keys to *personal reliability.*

So, it's time for you to take a look at yourself. How reliable are you? After all, you must understand and exhibit reliability before you can expect it from others on your team.

Your Say/Do Ratio

Reliable people have a high say/do ratio. That's the ratio of things you say you will do to the things you follow through on and do. In a perfect world, your say/do ratio is 1:1, meaning you have done everything that you said you would do. The reliable person has a rhythm of *say, do, say, do, say, do.* Keeping your word or simply doing the right thing is rarely convenient, but reliable people let their actions rise above their excuses.

Simply being aware of your say/do ratio can help change your behavior – improving your follow-through and more cautiously making promises.

Common, harmless statements we all often hear include: "I'll call you later," "I'll bring that article in for you," "Let's have lunch sometime," "I'll see if I can find that email and forward it to you," or "I'll follow up next week." They too often are just that – statements with no sense of personal promise behind them.

Reliable people do what they say. It seems so simple and at such a low bar to be reliable. You might ask whether people even remember all those little promises. They might not, but be assured they do notice when you deliver on them. When someone always follows through, it is impressive. It is the quickest way to build credibility and trust with others.

If you want to have a high say/do ratio, really think about your words. When you are about to say something that you will do, stop and ask yourself, "Do I really intend to act on this?" If the answer is "no," then just don't say it. Talk is cheap, but actions are like gold.

Being reliable does not mean saying "yes" to everyone. On the contrary, reliable people use discretion when they make commitments because they consider their commitments as personal promises to others. However, most people tend to slip on their commitments because they overestimate their available free time, want to please others, have unclear priorities and lack guiding principles for when to say "yes" or "no" to requests.

Natural barriers to negotiating achievable expectations include common human needs to please others, be accepted by them, be viewed as competent, be liked and to avoid conflict. Unfortunately, these needs are short-term versus long-term, revolve around *my* needs versus *team* needs and reflect insecurity versus confidence. The following four aspects of personal reliability address these barriers:

- Know yourself

- Know your priorities

- Manage timelines vs. deadlines

- Speak the language of reliability

When all is said and done,
more is said than done.

– AESOP,
Greek storyteller and
author, Aesop's Fables

Know Yourself

The most valuable type of knowledge is self-knowledge. Knowing your tendencies, preferences, values, personal limits, natural gifts and weaknesses helps you make the right commitments and keep them.

Aside from personal introspection, a good way to learn about yourself is to capture data on how others perceive you. For example, regularly ask your team what you can "Start, Stop and Keep" doing to be a better leader and support their success. You can have a "Start, Stop and Keep" discussion after finishing a project, wrapping up a meeting or during a scheduled review.

Another important aspect of self-knowledge is to have a clearly thought out set of personal values, a few things that are vital to you and reflect your uniqueness. For example, Lee's personal values are to *respect, serve* and *equip* others. Your values should dictate your decisions and behavior, not your circumstances or fleeting feelings. Being a reliable person not only means doing what you say, it also means doing what is right, regardless of what you have committed to.

Julie recently attended a session to help students prepare for college, and more importantly, for life. The presenter encouraged students to make early decisions about many things going forward, not just the university they choose. Some of these areas included making early decisions about the vision that they have for their future, what it will take to realize their vision and how they will handle difficult decisions. Since similar decisions lie ahead for each of us, making early decisions now can make the future much easier by:

- Removing the stress and pressure of making decisions "in the moment."

- Being comfortable that your decisions are aligned with your values and vision for your life.

- Ensuring clear thinking about consequences of decisions – good or bad (i.e., consider today what this action/decision will feel like in five hours, five days and five years).

Making early decisions increases the likelihood that you will realize your vision for a project, task, career, family, etc. To this day, Julie honors two early decisions she made in third grade – not to drink coffee or smoke cigarettes. She did not like the smell of the combination of coffee and smoke, so Julie decided to avoid these many years before they were even an option for her. That commitment made it easy to avoid coffee and cigarettes for her entire life. This early decision provided freedom for her and required little thought or energy at future decision points.

In which areas of your life can you make early decisions? Your values, your relationships, your leadership, your faith, your education, your health, your career, your legacy. It's never too late to make an early decision. Early decisions help pave the path to your desired future, whether you are in third grade, college or mid-career. Think about the future for you and your team. Make an early decision today to pave a smoother path for tomorrow and to help you become more personally reliable.

Observe all men; thyself most.

— BENJAMIN FRANKLIN,
U.S. founding father, author, printer,
political theorist, politician,
freemason, postmaster, scientist,
inventor, and diplomat

Know Your Priorities

In addition to knowing yourself, having clarity about your priorities also predicts your personal reliability. The most important decision in business, and in life, is to decide what's most important. So, as a request or an opportunity arises, ask yourself if this is a high priority for you. If it is a low priority for you today, what will really change to move it up to a high priority tomorrow? Ask for time to think about it and check your schedule. Reluctant or forced commitments, primarily those outside of work, typically result in lose-lose situations.

Our time, energy and money are precious resources in that once we spend them, we do not get them back to spend somewhere else. Therefore, saying "yes" to one task always means saying "no" to something else. We must say "no" to lower-value tasks in order to say "yes" to what is most important. To be personally reliable, avoid non-committal answers like "maybe." Be clear and direct. Redefine the term "polite" by taking the long view. You might be appeasing the other party by saying "yes" now, but you will ultimately disappoint them (and yourself) by overcommitting and possibly not delivering on your word. In today's non-committal and less reliable world, "yes" has become the new "maybe." If your "yes" really means "yes," you immediately vault into the top 5 percent of reliable people.

Making early decisions about your priorities provides a double benefit for boosting your personal reliability. For example, you might say that your order of priorities for how you spend your time might be family, work, friends and community. Making that early decision about your priorities would make it easier to say "yes" to spending your time with your higher priorities and occasionally say "no" to requests for lower priorities. The same would hold true for spending money. Let's say your top priorities are to spend on items that have a long-term benefit like retirement savings and experiences your family can share. It becomes clear that you might say "no" to a new couch if it forces you to say "no" to your 401(k) or a family vacation.

Don't think that saying "no" just means saying it to other people. Reliable people also say "no" to themselves – they sacrifice today (by saying "no" to something that might be fun or tempting) to achieve tomorrow's rewards (saying "yes" to their ultimate goal). Knowing when to say "no" is not a once-in-a-while thing; it's a daily action. For example, if you spend two hours in a meeting that doesn't help your team achieve its goals, you pay an opportunity cost by spending time on tasks that do not support your commitments. If you find yourself saying, "That was a waste of time," "Boy, that didn't add any value," or

"Why was I attending that meeting?"– these questions may be signs you need to say "no." Reliable people consistently ask themselves, "Is this the best invest-ment of my team's attention at this moment?" If it is, they get busy. If it's not, they refocus their attention.

Dwight D. Eisenhower, the World War II general who went on to become a popular president of the United States, used what is now called the *Eisenhower Method* for setting priorities. After identifying the tasks confronting him, he drew a square and divided it into four quadrants. One axis was a scale of important to unimportant; the other was urgent to not urgent. Tasks that fell into the *unimportant/not urgent* quadrant were dropped. Tasks in the *important/urgent* sector were accomplished immediately and by Ike personally. Tasks in the *unimportant/urgent* quadrant were delegated, and those in the *important/not urgent* quadrant were assigned due dates and done personally.

	Important	Unimportant
Urgent	Do It	Delegate It
Not Urgent	Defer It	Dump It

When using this model, distinguish between "urgent" and "important" activities. Something that's important is something that is beneficial and should be accomplished – if not right away, then eventually. Something that's urgent is time sensitive but not necessarily crucial.

As you identify priorities, be realistic about what you can accomplish and be honest with yourself about what you truly want to achieve in your life and work. Where do you want to invest your precious resources? Although important tasks are your top priorities, they will rarely appear urgent. *Don't be fooled into thinking that whatever seems urgent is worth taking your mind off your most important priority.* This is particularly challenging in today's world of instant information being pushed to your handheld device. Just because it appears in front of you does not mean it is important. Eisenhower's mantra was, "What's important is seldom urgent, and what's urgent is seldom important."

The sun provides a useful illustration of focus. It emits 3.8×10^{26} watts of power every second.[2] Add 24 zeros to the end of that number, and you'll get an idea of how much energy that is. However, with the sun's immense amount of energy, we can deflect most of its harmful effects with an ultra-thin application of sunscreen and a visor. On the other hand, a laser beam focusing only a few kilowatts of energy can cut a diamond in half or even eradicate certain types of cancer. Keeping laser-like clarity on your priorities boosts your personal reliability.

The key is not to prioritize what's on your schedule, but to schedule your priorities.

– STEPHEN R. COVEY,
author, *The 7 Habits of Highly Effective People*

Manage Timelines vs. Deadlines

We live in a world that trains us to meet deadlines, starting in grade school: Your paper is due May 15; college applications are due Oct. 1; finish your community service hours by Aug. 1; taxes are due April 15; the budget is due Nov. 15; your annual goals are due Jan. 15; your payment is due by Feb. 1. Deadlines, deadlines, deadlines.

Reliable people focus on timelines (when work gets done) to meet deadlines (when work is due). It is common to think that a task will take less time than it actually takes, so why not increase your estimate to ensure it will fit within your existing commitments? It is better to under-promise and over-deliver. If you make a promise that you can't keep because of truly terrible or unforeseen circumstances, let the person know as soon as possible. Be proactive. Bite the bullet and do not wait until the last minute to tell the other party you cannot do it. If you are late, call ahead to let the person know when you will arrive instead of letting him/her wonder where you are. This shows respect for others' time and preserves your credibility.

Paul Spiegelman is the former CEO of The Beryl Companies and Chief Culture Officer of Stericycle. He has found a healthy balance between reliability and the award-winning culture he has stewarded at his booming company. Spiegelman explains, "We don't like surprises. It's okay to give a leader a heads-up – that shows you are managing to timelines. But if you don't give a heads-up and you miss the deadline, then you are just managing deadlines."[3]

⭐

The greatest ability is dependability.

– BOB JONES, SR.,
evangelist and pioneer religious broadcaster

⭐

Speak the Language of Reliability

Your words speak the truth. They reflect your commitments – your promises to act. Whether you have a long conversation with a friend or a business conversation with a work colleague, every word makes a difference. The results of our interactions are rarely neutral; they are almost always positive or negative. Do my words reflect my commitment to be a reliable friend, spouse, sibling, or leader?

Words are the seeds of commitment. Reliable people see their words as their personal promises to others. Once they are spoken, your words either grow in the form of an immediate response, or they take time to germinate.

It's all too easy to let our personal reliability slip through the language we use. The power of your actions is preceded by the power of your words. Speaking with specificity creates a sense of reliability and commitment. Ambiguity is the Achilles heel of reliability. Ambiguous language increases frustration and rework, but specific language boosts reliability. It is the bridge to winning performance. Without this bridge, you are dead in the water. With it, you have the necessary platform to raise the reliability standard for yourself and your team. Build reliability for others and yourself by using specific phrases like these:

- Yes, I will do that for you.

- I'm not sure, but I'll give you a firm answer by noon tomorrow.

- I will own this.

- I will make time to get this done.

- I promise to close the loop by noon tomorrow so we can proceed.

- It will be done by Friday, March 18 at 2 p.m. Central Time.

At the same time, replace "reliability killers" like these because they sap energy and commitment:

- We'll see.

- I'll try.

- If I have the time.

- I will get back to you on that.

- Maybe.

- I'll do my best.

- When I get around to it.

Assess your own language of reliability by writing down common phrases you frequently say and write in your communications. Next, look at the language you have written down. Is it as specific as you want your team's language to be? Where can you be more specific? Do you use certain catch phrases that might not have specific and consistent meaning to others? Do your words reflect your personal promise to be reliable?

One of the classic lines from *Star Wars: The Empire Strikes Back* was delivered by Yoda, the Jedi Master: "Do … or do not. There is no try." If this 900-year-old little green guy can speak the language of reliability, so can you.

In an age when much more is being written than spoken, appreciation for the tone of the written word is being lost. For example, a typical cryptic text or email relies on emojis to communicate a serious, sarcastic or playful tone. Even the craftiest emoji user loses subtle intended meaning. When you are speaking, the words you stress can change the underlying meaning of a sentence.

Look at the following sentence: *I don't think he should get the job.* This simple sentence can have many levels of meaning based on the word you stress. Consider the meaning of the following sentences with the stressed word in **bold**. Read each sentence aloud and strongly stress the word in **bold**:

1. **I** don't think he should get the job.
   Meaning: *Somebody else thinks he should get the job.*

2. I **don't** think he should get the job.
   Meaning: *It's not true that I think he should get the job.*

3. I don't **think** he should get the job.
   Meaning: *That's not really what I mean. OR I'm not sure he'll get the job.*

4. I don't think **he** should get the job.
   Meaning: *Somebody else should get the job.*

5. I don't think he **should** get the job.
   Meaning: *In my opinion, it's wrong that he's going to get the job.*

6. I don't think he should **get** the job.
   Meaning: *He should have to earn (be worthy of, work hard for) the job.*

7. I don't think he should get **the** job.
   Meaning: *He should get another job.*

8. I don't think he should get the **job**.
   Meaning: *Maybe he should get something else instead.*

As you can see, this simple eight-word sentence can be interpreted eight different ways, resulting in very unreliable communication. Today's information-rich, time-poor world forces us to write and speak more specifically and clearly than ever. If we do not, we are rolling the dice. We have just a one-in-eight, or

12.5 percent, chance that others will receive the same simple message we are sending.

Excellent leaders start with their own reliability before they expect it from their teams. The positive example they provide sets the expectation for their teams to also deliver reliable performance. So, let's explore the five coaching habits that excellent leaders use to achieve reliable team performance.

Promises are the uniquely human way of ordering the future, making it predictable and reliable to the extent that this is humanly possible.

— HANNAH ARENDT,
political theorist and philosopher

★

Watch your thoughts;
> *they become your words.*

Watch your words;
> *they become your actions.*

Watch your actions;
> *they become your habits.*

Watch your habits;
> *they become your character.*

Watch your character;
> *it becomes your destiny.*

— FRANK OUTLAW,
founder, BI-LO supermarket chain

★

Keys to Personal Reliability

- Know yourself.

- Know your priorities.

- Manage timelines vs. deadlines.

- Speak the language of reliability.

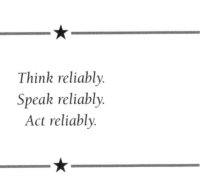

Think reliably.
Speak reliably.
Act reliably.

★ Taking Action ★

Personal Reliability

1. What are my top two work priorities?

2. How can I use my knowledge of my priorities to better manage my commitments?

3. What are my two most common responses when someone asks me to do something?

4. Do these words reflect a personal promise to be reliable? If not, how can I adjust my language?

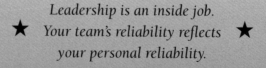

Leadership is an inside job.
★ *Your team's reliability reflects* ★
your personal reliability.

Coaching
RELIABILITY

---★---

*Leaders are sculptors. They might not shape marble,
but they shape something much more precious:
people's lives.*

---★---

Reliability is something every leader wants more of from his or her team. Your challenge is to coach for reliable individual performance as the building block of a reliable and profitable business. Jeanne Bliss, an expert on customer-driven growth, discusses the power of social media to amplify your experience with any given business, good or bad:

When you deliver a reliable experience, you earn the right to your customers' story through word of mouth. And your customers will come back because they want to have that experience again. There are three repeated points that customers talk about through social media, which will earn you the right to new customer growth without the acquisition cost and organic growth of your existing customers. These are:

1. *Was the experience consistent and reliable, no matter where or whom the customer talked to in any channel?*

2. *Does their relationship with you improve their life or business? Did your actions prove your commitment to them?*

> *3. How does it feel for the customer to do business*
> *with you? Honored, distrusted, ignored?*[1]

Of course, on the contrary, when the customer experience is unreliable, word-of-mouth referrals decline or disappear. Reliability is a customer magnet, whereas unreliability is a customer deterrent.

When a customer needs something done by a set date, or a service performed in a specific manner, he's seeking someone who can provide that service with certainty. Many companies have built their reputations by providing that certainty for customers. For example, FedEx realized it could corner the market by promising to get your letter to its destination overnight, without fail. The company created an entire niche that never existed before. McDonald's has built its iconic brand based on a promise of a reliable experience, regardless of which location.

Andrew Carnegie was an excellent leader and coach. He came to America from his native Scotland when he was a small boy, did a variety of odd jobs, and eventually ended up as the largest steel manufacturer in the United States. At one time, he was the wealthiest man in America. To put his wealth into perspective, he built Pittsburgh's Carnegie Steel Company, which he sold to J.P. Morgan in 1901 for $480 million. Today's equivalent value is nearly $400 billion. He was also a great philanthropist, donating the current equivalent of $79 billion to various charities, universities and libraries. At one point, he had 43 millionaires working for him. In the late 1800s, a millionaire was a very rare person.

A reporter asked Carnegie how he had hired 43 millionaires. Carnegie responded that those men had not been millionaires when they started working for him but had become millionaires as a result. The reporter's next question was, "How did you develop these men to become so valuable to you that you have paid them this much money?" Carnegie replied that men are developed the same way gold is mined. When gold is mined, several tons of dirt must be moved to get an ounce of gold, but one doesn't go into the mine looking for dirt – one goes in looking for the gold.

Some leaders find themselves sitting on a mountain of gold while feeling poor because they don't know how to mine the gold from their teams. Excellent leaders go in looking for gold; once they find it, they coach their teams to refine the gold. Ultimately, excellent leaders help good employees become even better *people*. They help their employees build better lives for themselves and others while producing better business results.

There are five habits that excellent coaches use to create the reliability advantage. The five habits give your team the biggest boost if applied in sequence. However, you must use your knowledge of your team to determine when to accelerate through or spend more time on a specific habit.

The root meaning of the verb "to coach" means to bring a person from where they are to where they want to be. Consider the role of a football coach. He sets clear expectations for his team with a game plan to win. He asks players if they have any questions to ensure they are clear about their respective roles on the team. He also asks them questions like, "How can you improve your performance or overcome a certain obstacle?" Then during the game, he involves them in changing the game plan, if necessary, based on what they are seeing on the field. The coach also observes and measures each player's performance (e.g., number of tackles, yards gained, etc.). Finally, the coach gives constructive feedback and recognition so his players can elevate their performance in the next game.

These are the same five habits that excellent leaders employ to coach their teams. First, excellent leaders *explain expectations*. They realize it is necessary but not sufficient, in and of itself, to boost performance. Excellent leaders take the time to ensure alignment with their teams before moving forward. Second, excellent leaders also *ask questions*. A leader might ask to clarify a problem or ask for ideas and suggestions. Asking questions ignites employee engagement. Third, excellent coaches *involve team members* in creating solutions to improve their work. This enlists ownership because we are committed to things we help create. Fourth, excellent leaders diligently *measure results* to boost team accountability. The fifth and final coaching habit is to *appreciate people*. This builds commitment to sustain and improve results. Using each of these habits in concert elevates team reliability.

The 5 Coaching Habits

1 EXPLAIN
Expectations ➡ Alignment

2 ASK
Questions ➡ Engagement

3 INVOLVE
Team ➡ Ownership

4 MEASURE
Results ➡ Accountability

5 APPRECIATE
People ➡ Commitment

The left side of this model shows five coaching habits that drive reliable performance. This is the *side of choice*. Each day, leaders choose whether to take these actions. Their choices influence the right side of the model – the *results*. If you choose your habits, then you must take responsibility for your results. You are each responsible for the choices you make and the results you ultimately achieve. If you choose *not* to build these coaching habits, you must accept these predictable outcomes:

- Instead of Alignment, you get Confusion

- Instead of Engagement, you get Disengagement

- Instead of Ownership, you get Entitlement

- Instead of Accountability, you get Blame

- Instead of Commitment, you get Compliance

These coaching habits are based on natural human dynamics and needs. That's why it does not look like rocket science and seems so simple. That is also the reason why these habits work across generations, industries and cultures – because they meet human needs in the workplace. It is easy for one thing or another to get in the way of these habits, but if you say "yes" to those things, you are saying "no" to reliable team performance. Coaching for reliable performance is not a "salt and pepper" practice. You cannot sprinkle on a little *explaining* here and *appreciation* there and expect *reliability*. You must perform these habits consistently. If world-class athletes need a coach every day, why wouldn't your team?

Each day you are making a choice about your team's alignment, engagement, ownership, accountability and commitment. Let's see how a team leader, Lexi, and an employee, Cameron, progress through the five coaching habits to boost reliability:

> **Lexi:** "Hey, Cameron. I'm glad I bumped into you. I wanted to talk to you about something. We really need to improve our response time on special orders. If we do, we will create a positive ripple effect with our core customer, which will drive sales, and that's good for all of us." (*Lexi is explaining expectations and consequences.*)

> **Cameron:** "OK, I understand." (*Cameron is simply observing.*)

> **Lexi:** "You're on the front lines with this issue. Why do you think our response time has increased lately?" (*Lexi is asking questions.*)

> **Cameron:** "Well, the new system migration has had its bumps. But I think the bigger issue is that we weren't prepared for the recent promotional campaign for our VIP customers. Our call volume from VIPs has increased by 80% for special orders

over the same period last quarter."
(*Cameron is becoming engaged.*)

Lexi: "We need to discuss your ideas on how we can get back on track. Our response time has a direct impact on our bottom line, so I'll give you whatever support you need to take care of this." (*Lexi is involving Cameron.*)

Cameron: "That sounds great. Let me get some input from my team and send you some recommendations before our meeting. I'm confident we can identify a good solution and implement it quickly." (*Now Cameron is owning the solution.*)

Lexi: (*after they meet*) "I like your recommendations, Cameron. Let's measure the key metrics you identified each week for the next month and touch base to see if we need to tweak anything." (*Lexi is observing performance and providing feedback along the way.*)

Cameron: (*next month*) "Looks like we are in good shape. Our response time has gone down each week, and we have been at our target of 20 percent reduction in response time for the past two weeks. How about if I just keep an eye on things now and send you a quick scorecard each month to ensure we sustain the changes?" (*Cameron is taking accountability for the results.*)

Lexi: "That sounds great, Cameron. I am really impressed with how you took control of this challenge, involved your team and executed the solution. I really appreciate your efforts. Well done!" (*Lexi is appreciating Cameron and his performance.*)

Since Lexi applied the five coaching habits, Cameron is feeling a sense of personal commitment to his job and to his leader. Plus, he is motivated to perform reliably so he can be reinforced by his leader again, because it feels good. We all like to be reinforced for our performance.

Of course, even on the most reliable teams, there will be instances when you must find leadership courage to address performance problems. Elaine Agather is Chairman of Dallas Region JPMorgan Chase and head of its Private Bank. She is a beloved and direct leader who understands the responsibility of her role. Agather states, "The team is bigger than any issue at hand. The leader has a personal accountability to the team to have tough conversations and to occasionally make tough decisions with individuals."[2]

Excellent leaders such as Agather choose to meet the needs of their teams over any personal discomfort. It reminds us of our son's former high school football coach, Chris Cunningham, who would preach this same leadership concept of "team over me" with this visual he had printed on T-shirts:

TEAM
me

Reliability is a two-way street. You get reliable performance from your team by being a reliable leader for them. Additionally, excellent leaders do not use the five habits as separate leadership tools. Instead, they integrate the coaching habits into their daily interactions, realizing it is the most effective way to create the reliability advantage. Let's take a closer look at each of the five coaching habits and how you can create the reliability advantage for your team.

Simplicity is prerequisite for reliability.

– EDSGER W. DIJKSTRA,
computer science research pioneer

Coaching Habit #1

EXPLAIN
Expectations  **Alignment**

Unclear expectations lead to unclear destinations.

At the most basic level, the job of a leader is to equip team members with knowledge and tools to be successful. A leader is only successful if his/her team is successful. That includes educating team members on organizational systems like budgeting, goal setting, authority levels for spending and training. The leader must also educate his team on informal "learning the ropes" things like company culture norms during working hours, lunchtime, meetings etiquette, attire, how presentations are made, key people to keep in the loop and how decisions are really made, regardless of what a policy states. Equipping your team by explaining these aspects of the job is not a one-time thing you check off your leadership list. Excellent leaders continually explain, educate and equip their team with tips, tools, training and insights.

Reliable performance starts at the beginning of the performance process. If we wait until the end, then we are simply imposing consequences rather than inspiring positive performance. That's why aligning on expectations is the foundation for reliable team performance.

Expectation gaps lead to execution gaps. The large majority of performance frustrations stem from not communicating clear expectations up front. Therefore, the coaching key is to front-end-load reliability. You and your team should be able to easily align on the answer to this question: "How will I know if I have met expectations?" We cannot rely on others' perceptions of our expectations. The imperfect nature of human communication requires us to be more specific than we think we need to be. Lack of clear expectations is the most common reason for performance problems. There is not really a close second. Gaining alignment through clear expectations is job No. 1 for excellent leaders.

The Fundamental Four

To gain alignment, explain your answers to the fundamental four questions. These are questions that every employee asks, regardless of whether you hear them:

1. Where are we going? (Goals)

2. What are we doing to get there? (Plans)

3. How can I contribute? (Roles)

4. What's in it for me? (Rewards)

Like any aspect of leadership, gaining alignment does not just happen. It must be intentional. Our late friend and excellent leader Ron Rossetti liked to say, "Awesomeness is never accidental." Our clients who paint a clear picture for their teams are intentional about answering the fundamental four questions. They use the questions as a checklist to ensure that the content of significant company communications address each question. The alignment in their organizations is notably greater and their results are notably more reliable. Answering the fundamental four creates a bridge that connects today's tasks to the broader team purpose.

Excellent leaders help their teams see and understand the longer-term, downstream impact of their personal performance on team results, on the organization, on customers, on shareholders and ultimately on themselves (what's in it for me?). When employees see how their actions help or hinder others, it aligns their performance with clear consequences. The personal impact to an employee might include opportunities for promotions, development, exposure to executives, public recognition, expanded responsibilities, flexibility in the job, oversight of others, ownership of projects and/or financial rewards.

In addition to *formal* communication, explain expectations for your team with each *informal* communication – walking in the hallway, popping into their workspace to see how they are doing, etc. With today's information-overloaded workplace, it can be challenging to decide what to communicate to employees and what to withhold. It's easy to say (usually to ourselves), "They don't really need to know all that," or, "My team won't really understand," or, "I don't think they can handle that news right now." But be cautious because those who *under*estimate the intelligence of others tend to *over*estimate their own.

When employees don't get the necessary information to perform their jobs, including the answers to the fundamental four, they tend to "fill in the blanks" with their own assumptions, and their assumptions are often worst-case scenarios. This is not necessarily a reflection of the leader. It's our natural human insecurity. We often assume the worst in the absence of evidence to the contrary. Lack of information and unanswered questions can start the *silence spiral*:

Silence leads to doubt;

   Doubt leads to fear;

      Fear leads to panic;

         Panic leads to worst-case thinking.

The silence spiral undermines trust and puts a damper on passion. It can take five minutes or five weeks to play out, but in most cases, it happens more rapidly than we would imagine. A closed office door, a vague reply to an honest question, an unreciprocated greeting as you pass in the hallway, or a canceled one-on-one meeting can all trigger the silence spiral.

Prevent the silence spiral by proactively explaining expectations. Nothing compares to hearing the facts directly from the boss. For example, if you learn about a new project or change that won't affect your team for a few months, go ahead and give them a heads-up now. They can start preparing, or at minimum, they won't be caught off guard or be inclined to listen to and perpetuate rumors. Excellent leaders realize they are not really protecting their teams by keeping them in the dark. Employees will either find out on their own or may make assumptions that are worse than reality. More importantly, silence chips away at trust and your leadership credibility. So, use every interaction, meeting and communication to explain expectations.

The 3 W's

Excellent leaders help their teams by clearly and specifically defining the actions, timing and results they expect from others and from themselves. For each member of your team, make certain you communicate the 3W's (What, Who and When).

What	Who	When	Status/Comments
1.			
2.			
3.			

We use a very similar format with our coaching clients to help them drive millions of dollars in improvement. The power is in its simplicity. To ensure clear expectations when using the 3W form, identify only one "Who" per action. This will avoid "two-headed monsters" since a "We" is unowned and undone. This simple 3W form is even more powerful when you carry it with you as a mental template to bring closure to daily conversations and interactions.

Although aligning on clear expectations can be tedious, if you take the necessary time to do it, you will end up spending less time dealing with performance problems and more time executing your plan. A broad and persuasive series of studies confirms that *specificity of goals* dramatically increases the likelihood of success. For example, in one study, participants were asked to write a report on how they spent Christmas Eve, and then to write that report within two days after Christmas Eve. Half of the participants were required to specify when and where within those two days they intended to write the report. The other half was not required to give specifics. Among those who had to provide specifics, 71 percent handed the reports in on time. Only 32 percent of the second group did so.[1]

Prevent Re-coaching

When our son was 11 years old, he earned his junior black belt in karate. Of course, we were very proud of him, for he had come a very long way since his first lesson. We remember that lesson well. He was 7 years old, and one of the first things the master instructor taught him was a simple exercise called a kata. This kata ended with him, the beginning student, saying emphatically, "V for victory and bow for humility" as he crisscrossed arms over his head with fists clinched for the "V" and then bowed for humility.

That night, he came home from his lesson and quickly ran to us to proudly show us what he had learned. Seeing his enthusiasm, we dropped what we were doing and became an intent audience of two. As he finished the kata, he performed the closing, "V for victory, bow for humility!" he shouted. But then, to our surprise, he started yelling insults at us … "Man,

I took you down! How about that, buddy?" and so on. More than a bit shocked and confused, we asked, "Hey pal, what was *that* all about?" He responded in a very matter-of-fact manner, "That's the bow for humility."

Well, this pointed out how such a little difference could make a BIG difference – he thought it was a bow for *humiliation*, not humility! Fear not. We clarified that definition before he earned his black belt. If we depend on others' perceptions to meet our expectations, we will be disappointed. Our son heard his instructor's performance expectation but made his own (incredibly misdirected) interpretation based on his own perceptions. The truth is we remember only 20 percent of what we hear.

Why is this percentage so low? Let's say you are hurried and swing by an employee's cube and say, "Grace, please make sure you use the new format on the month-end sales report … thanks." Even if Grace is a sharp employee, what do you think the chances are she will hear your request accurately, remember it, recall it accurately when it's relevant, interpret your instructions as you intended, then perform the task satisfactorily? When we look at it this way, 20 percent sounds good.

Explaining expectations up front minimizes re-coaching on the back end. If you are coaching employees on the same thing repeatedly, before you get frustrated with them, ask yourself, "Am I inspiring learning or am I just checking this off my list?" "Am I handing off a memo with instructions or am I asking the employee to perform a task while I give him real-time feedback?"

As this learning pyramid below illustrates, inspiring excellent performance requires time and effort. We generally remember:

10%
of what
we read
(memos, books – that's why we have chapter
summary pages to help increase your retention!)

20%
of what we hear
(instructions)

30% of what we see
(looking at pictures)

50% of what we hear and see
(watching a movie, looking at an exhibit,
watching a demonstration)

70% of what we say
(participating in a discussion, giving a talk)

90% of what we both say and do
(simulating the real thing, doing the real thing)

In the example with our son, he heard his performance expectation (20 percent chance of remembering) but made his own interpretations from there. Well, this happens on our teams every day, and it's up to us to ensure effective coaching of our teams. Explaining to gain alignment is a pay-me-now or pay-me-later leadership proposition. Take a shortcut and we will be saying the same thing to the same employee next week – no fun for either of us. Create a habit of aligning on expectations to boost your team's reliability.

The **5** Coaching Habits

1 EXPLAIN
Expectations ➡ **Alignment**

- Answer the Fundamental Four questions (goals, plans, roles and rewards)

- Align on the 3W's – What, Who and When.

- Coach UP your team by moving DOWN the learning pyramid.

★

People can't live up to the expectations they don't know have been set for them.

– RORY VADEN,
author, *Take the Stairs*

★

★ Taking Action ★

EXPLAIN
Expectations ━━━━▶ Alignment

1. How can I intentionally share my team's goals, plans, roles and rewards (i.e., answer to the fundamental four questions) in my daily interactions and meetings?

2. How can I institutionalize the use of the 3W's (What, Who, When) as a follow-up to our meetings?

3. How can I adjust my approach to explaining expectations to push down the learning pyramid and prevent re-coaching?

★ *We must explain the game plan to win the game.* ★

Coaching Habit #2

ASK
Questions  **Engagement**

*Questions are the golden keys that unlock
hearts and minds.*

— Bob Tiede,
author, *Great Leaders Ask Questions*

Explaining expectations is the first coaching habit of excellent leaders, but explaining is only a one-way process. To continue building reliable performance, ask questions to initiate two-way communication and engage your team. Coaching is more about asking questions than it is about knowing the answers. Managers *tell* while coaches *ask*. Business schools don't teach courses on asking questions, so leaders rarely, if ever, study questions the way they would study a financial report. Additionally, most leadership training focuses on solving problems and identifying solutions, but excellent leaders also focus on asking questions. This skill better engages teams, and it also takes the pressure off the leader to know all the answers.

Questions are really the answer. Asking questions is a long-established practice to demonstrate respect, diffuse tense situations, obtain buy-in and make employees feel valued in a way that financial rewards cannot. Questions either expand or limit the solutions and creativity to seize opportunities and solve problems.

Last summer we enjoyed a family trip to Greece. It is a land of boundless beauty and tremendous thinkers. While touring the Acropolis, our guide mentioned that while scheduling its restoration, time was built into each day for workers to spend time thinking! Imagine that happening almost anywhere else in the world. Greece's history is built upon the minds of the world's greatest thinkers. One of them is Greek philosopher Socrates. Even though he's nearly 2,500 years our senior we are still on a first-name basis. Okay, he only had one name.

Today, Socrates is alive and well in excellent leaders. His Socratic method of questioning is a timely and timeless leadership tool for engaging teams and challenging thought processes. Asking questions is both selfless and self-serving. It demonstrates interest in your team while providing you with insights into their motivations, passions, challenges, assumptions, and aspirations. The next time you are tempted to tell your team what to do, take a lesson from Socrates and ask what they think instead.

Purposeful Questions

Plenty of books are filled with lists of questions, but asking questions without a clear objective is like playing the question lotto. Very occasionally you might get lucky and win, but most of the time you will come up empty-handed. That's a loss for you and for your team member. There is rarely a right answer to a wrong question.

There are four main reasons to ask questions: to understand, assess, innovate and motivate. It is important to understand your objectives before you start asking. Within each objective, your question might focus on the person or the project/process. For example, if you want to understand, most leaders jump directly to questions that help them understand their team's *projects* and *processes* by asking:

- What's the goal?

- What's the plan?

- What are your options?

However, excellent leaders start with questions to help understand their *people*, such as:

- In which areas would you like to grow?

- What do you love to do?

- What do you need to be at your very best?

Showing genuine interest in your employees as people is the foundation of a fully engaged team. Theodore Roosevelt summed it up nicely when he said, "People don't care how much you know until they know how much you care." If you need to motivate your people to action, you might ask:

- What needs to happen for this to succeed?

- What do you think the next steps should be?

- What's in it for you and the team if this is wildly successful?

Certain coaching questions work in almost any situation. These are some of our favorites that we have heard excellent leaders ask:

- What do *you* think?

- Why do you think this is happening?

- What can we *start, stop and keep* to improve?

- And what else? (Repeated as a prompt to obtain more details.)

- Is this your very best work? (Lee's mentor asks him this!)

A table on the next page serves as a guide to keep your coaching questions purposeful.

Asking Purposeful Questions

UNDERSTAND To gain knowledge and solicit insights	ASSESS To determine options and make decisions
The Person • In which areas would you like to grow? • What do you love to do? • What do you need to be at your very best? • What would you like to be doing in three years? • How can we more fully utilize your skills? • What are you really passionate about? • What's your "why," your core motivation for working?	**The Person** • What would you change if you were in my position? • What's the most important thing you can accomplish today? • Which option makes the most sense to you? • What are the consequences of the choices? • What does your gut tell you? • What one thing could you improve to elevate your game?
The Project / Process • What's the goal? • What is your plan? • What are the alternative choices being considered? • What's the current situation? • What would you need to make this project succeed? • Who are the key players on your team? • Who are the stakeholders?	**The Project / Process** • What is your next step? • What conclusions have you reached so far? • What's the biggest risk? • What are the key factors in making this decision? • What is conflicting with your most important priorities? • How can we collect 80% of the data we need in the shortest time possible?

INNOVATE To generate ideas and improve methods	**MOTIVATE** To achieve a goal and implement a plan
The Person • What would you do if funds were unlimited? • What would you do differently if you had no fear of failing? • When do you feel the most creative? • Who do you brainstorm the best with? • What's one thing you would change today? • What do you think our business will look like in 10 years?	**The Person** • What needs to happen for this to succeed? • What do you think the next steps should be? • What's in it for you and the team if this is wildly successful? • How can I best help or support you? • How can we maintain focus and excitement? • Do we have the right people in the right roles to ensure success?
The Project / Process • What if we looked at this from a totally different perspective? • How could we do this in half the time? • Who does this process better than anyone in the world? • Which steps do not add value to our customer? • What is one more alternative to consider?	**The Project / Process** • What barriers do you need removed? • How will we know if we are successful? • What are the key milestones we must hit to stay on track? • What are a few quick wins we can achieve and celebrate? • What is the accountability process? • What's going well so far?

The Sound of Silence

Most people go to great lengths to avoid silence during conversations. They fill silence with anything, regardless of how meaningful (or meaningless). It is as if silence has its own gravitational force that pulls words from our mouths to prevent a single moment of silence. Of course, we have all experienced those three seconds of silence that felt like three minutes.

Excellent leaders not only know the right questions to ask, but they also know how to patiently wait for an answer. They are comfortable with silence. If you are not comfortable with the silence, you will fill it with another question that leaves your original question unanswered and squelches engagement. After asking an employee a question, your patience creates power. Resist the gravitational pull to fill the void. Your silence creates accountability for a response. You would rather wait for a well-thought-out response than get a quick, half-baked reply.

Blind Spots

All the questions in the world will not help your team if you are not listening. You don't learn when you're talking; you learn when you're listening. Excellent coaches are also excellent listeners and learners. Mark Twain said, "If we were supposed to talk more than we listen, we would have two mouths and one ear." If you're not listening to your employees, you will gradually suffer from "blind spots" – weaknesses that are apparent to others but not to you.

A classic episode of *Seinfeld* featured Elaine while she was the acting president of her company. She couldn't figure out why her entire staff was suddenly shying away from her. She quickly blamed her friend George for her seeming downfall at the office. This all started to happen after a company party where Elaine, thinking she was a good dancer, did not hesitate to show off a few of her moves. Unfortunately, this was a HUGE blind spot for Elaine. It was painfully clear to everyone else that Elaine was a horrible dancer as she flailed and contorted her way across the floor! When Jerry asked his friend George if Elaine danced at the party, George replied, "It was more like a full-bodied dry heave set to music."[1] As a viewer, you could feel the sting of embarrassment for her and the dread if you should ever find yourself in such a situation. Fortunately for Elaine, she had an incredibly blunt friend in Kramer who, in no uncertain terms, revealed her blind spot by responding to her request for feedback on her dancing with an emphatic, "You stink!"[2] Learn from Elaine. Listen to your employees, particularly your "Kramers."

Excellent leaders prevent blind spots by making concerted efforts to keep in tune with the realities of their employees – listening for the truth. This is particularly important because the higher you are in an organization, the more filtered the information you receive. It's a natural and predictable phenomenon, but it's also a precarious position for any leader. No leader wants to be "Elaine on the dance floor." Therefore, the higher your leadership position, the more listening you need to do.

By simply asking questions, your employees will reveal challenges and opportunities that could potentially take you months or years to identify. Asking questions and then really listening demonstrates personal respect, obtains buy-in, and makes people feel valued in a way that financial rewards cannot. Listen for the entire message your employee is communicating with his words, tone, posture, eyes, energy, hesitations, fluency, etc. Excellent leaders listen at least 50 percent of the time. Andrew Levi, a client and excellent leader of numerous businesses, has done a tremendous amount of leading, presenting, pitching, directing, persuading, and explaining in his efforts to build winning cultures and businesses. When asked about the topic of listening, he directly replied, "He who talks the most loses."[3] Ask, be silent and listen to engage your team.

The **5** Coaching Habits

1 EXPLAIN
Expectations  Alignment

2 ASK
Questions ⟹ Engagement

- Define your objective *before* you ask.

- Get comfortable with silence *after* you ask.

- After you ask, listen to eliminate your blind spots.

★

It is not the answer that enlightens,
but the question.

– EUGENE IONESCO,
playwright

★

★ Taking Action ★

ASK
Questions ➤ **Engagement**

1. How can I ensure that I am asking purposeful questions? (e.g., Before a meeting or team interaction, take a minute to define your objective, then use the table from this chapter to identify appropriate questions to ask.)

2. After I ask a question, what can I do to occupy my mind for up to 10 seconds to ensure I am not filling silence before my team member can respond? (e.g., count to 10)

 Engage employees with three simple steps: ask, listen and learn.

Coaching Habit #3

INVOLVE
Team

 **Ownership**

Tell me and I'll forget;
show me and I may remember;
involve me and I'll understand.

— Xun Kuang,
Confucian philosopher

For years, leaders at the top of many organizations often had more knowledge than those on the front-lines. Today, the game has changed. Technology has put knowledge in the hands of anyone with access to a computer or handheld device. Today, it's impossible for leaders to know it all. Plus, it is not in their own or in the organization's best interest to try. That's why you need to involve team members in finding solutions and innovations that boost product and service reliability for your customers.

By asking your employees questions, you engage in a two-way information exchange. To continue to create the reliability advantage, involve your team in improving its work process and output. Take the ideas your team gives you and involve them in developing solutions to problems, identifying areas for improvement and finding opportunities for growth.

People support what they help create. Ask team members to bring you solutions along with problems. By involving employees, you enlist their ownership of new issues and solve problems. Some leaders feel threatened by the idea of involving their employees in identifying and solving problems. They believe they're giving up control over *how* their team will achieve its goals. However, excellent leaders realize there is more than one way to solve a problem. An employee's approach might be different from the leader's, but the personal ownership that comes from being involved in the solution far outweighs any loss of control that a leader might feel.

Dashboard and Under-the-Hood Knowledge

A common misperception among leaders is that once you get to a certain level, you should consider only a 30,000-ft. perspective (i.e., big picture) of your business. Although a high-level perspective is necessary for leadership success, it must be accompanied by an in-depth understanding of your team's operation (e.g., your drivers of cost, profit, quality and customer satisfaction). When we make a habit of ignoring the little things, we eventually end up ignoring the big things. Don't misinterpret this as micromanagement. We are discussing leadership knowledge, not leadership activity.

Your car provides a helpful analogy for understanding the importance of both big picture and detailed information. Just as your car's dashboard tells you speed, fuel level and engine temperature, your organizational dashboard tells you if sales are up 5 percent, productivity is down or project deliverables are on schedule. Leaders typically use dashboard knowledge.

While dashboard knowledge is important for understanding broad metrics and the general direction of your operation, it is less helpful for identifying specific actions, improvements and adjustments that will help your team run more smoothly. For that kind of information, you have to look "under the hood." Looking under your car's hood provides insight into why your car is running hot, why it veers to the right, and why it's not starting as quickly as it should. Under-the-hood knowledge about your team gives you specific information with respect to a given job, time, place and set of circumstances.

Excellent leaders involve team members who possess under-the-hood knowledge. They understand that by the time a warning light on your dashboard starts blinking, you already have a problem under the hood. Your frontline team members then become your experts.

One of our clients, Bob Bunker, CEO of NeuLife Neurological Rehabilitation, likes to harken back to his military days when he's looking under the hood. He refers to his field offices as the FEBA (Forward Edge of Battle Area). It's a vivid reminder to his corporate team that the field offices are where the business battle is won on a daily basis. Bunker has been known to spend much of his time on the FEBA listening to his field team and customers and supporting them both. He says, "Getting on the FEBA allows me to see and feel the daily processes and ponder process reengineering opportunities and technology applications, and better appreciate the interdependencies of our corporate and customer systems as a whole."[1] Involving his frontline team gives Bunker a more complete view of his business and enlists team ownership of the solutions. Excellent leaders put their egos and past experiences aside to seek real-time input from team members who are working under the hood every day.

Involve to Improve

There is no doubt that five heads are better than one, so involve your team – your experts – in seeking new ways to reduce expenses, improve quality, expedite customer service or improve coordination with other departments. Employees will exchange their involvement for ownership in the outcomes. Their ideas will make their work more interesting and efficient. Involve your team members in solving problems – team problems or even their own performance problems. You know what they say ... the biggest room in the world is the room for improvement.

One of our long-standing clients, National Motor Club, is a provider of roadside assistance and other membership benefits for owners of autos and recreational vehicles. Their CEO at the time, Matt Krzysiak, rolled out an initiative called "The Dumb Things We Do." It was a lighthearted, non-threatening way to uncover goofy policies and inefficient processes that chipped away at customer loyalty, profit margins and employee engagement. Over the course of a week, employees submitted short descriptions of any activity they thought did not add value and should be stopped. All the feedback was compiled into a single list. Krzysiak shared the list with the entire company – with an open mind, no judgment and lots of laughs – to reinforce his team's courage in revealing these issues. Then he involved the employees in fixing or stopping "The Dumb Things We Do."

The biggest opportunity for improvement is typically with the skills on your team. Underutilized skills are hidden yet huge areas of waste. Start by appreciating that all employees are different and have different levels of potential. Just like your kids, you cannot view them as the same person with the same needs and potential. Excellent leaders do not try to make everyone achieve at the same level; rather, they see it as their mission to help each employee reach his/her potential. To do so, when you address specific performance problems with employees, involve them in identifying the root cause of the problem and solutions to enlist their ownership in reaching their potential. Also, refer to the previous *Ask Questions* chapter to help you involve employees in a discussion to improve their skills.

Define Team Involvement Roles

In today's increasingly complex business world, most organizational structures incorporate a matrix element. Gone are the days of traditional functional or divisional structures, particularly for businesses with multiple products/services and/or locations. "Managing the Matrix" is a way of life. Organization charts have more dotted lines than a Los Angeles freeway. So, collaboration has become a critical competency for today's reliable team. The word says it all: "co-labor," to work together.

Collaboration should not be confused (but often is) with consensus. Collaboration is a way of working together, whereas consensus is a form of decision-making. Allowing collaboration to morph into consensus leads to the similar dynamic of a trial jury. When all team members must agree in order to move forward, any one person can stall a decision. Sliding down the slippery slope of consensus will put the brakes on your team and halt forward progress. In a speed-craved marketplace, that's the kiss of death. Also, to collaborate well, team members must have clearly defined involvement roles. We suggest simple language and definitions that help your team focus on delivering reliable results:

- **Owner** – The person *ultimately responsible* for the completion of a project, and the one who assigns tasks and resources. There can be only one owner per project/initiative, and s/he makes final decisions.

- **Performer** – Those who *directly perform* the tasks. Executors collaborate with subject-matter experts, as needed.

- **Expert** – The person who *provides subject-matter expertise* as requested by the owner and performer. This typically involves two-way communication about best practices, customer needs and alternative approaches.

- **Stakeholder** – Those who are *kept up-to-date* on progress by owners and performers, often only on completion of milestones. This typically involves one-way communication with executive or peer stakeholders.

To involve your team in a collaborative way, you must let roles, not egos, drive actions. On any given project, a team member can play different roles. You might be getting informed on today's project and lead a team for next month's project. Clarify team involvement roles to enlist ownership in work process and outcomes.

Zig Ziglar had a famous quote: *You can get just about anything in life you want if you help enough other people get what they want.* This seems to hold true for team members. It's not about who gets the credit. It's not about who is the leader. It's about helping the other team members accomplish the goal. In that way, everyone is successful.

The 5 Coaching Habits

1 EXPLAIN
Expectations ➡️ **Alignment**

2 ASK
Questions ➡️ **Engagement**

3 INVOLVE
Team ➡️ **Ownership**

- Seek those with under-the-hood knowledge.

- Involve to improve.

- Define team involvement roles.

---★---

*When people are financially invested,
they want a return.*

*When people are emotionally invested,
they want to contribute.*

– SIMON SINEK,
author, *Start With Why*

---★---

★ Taking Action ★

INVOLVE
Team ⟶ Ownership

1. Who are my team members that possess under-the-hood knowledge?

2. How can I regularly seek their input and involve them in making improvements?

 Your team owns what they help create.

Coaching Habit #4

MEASURE
Results ➡ Accountability

What gets measured gets done.

— PETER DRUCKER,
pioneer of modern business practices

Have you ever noticed the intensity difference when you play a game for fun compared to "playing for keeps"? Our family and friends frequently play Ping-pong in our game room. It's a fun and easy game for all ages. We can see the Ping-pong table from our kitchen. When the players are just warming up, you notice their relaxed stance, the slow rhythmic sound of the ball hitting each paddle and then brief silence after a shot is missed. As soon as they start keeping score, there are visible changes. Each player is now slightly crouched down with eyes wide open looking straight ahead, the rhythm of the ball is faster and louder, and a missed shot is usually accompanied with a cheer or groan of agony. Scorekeeping generates greater intensity, better focus, more energy and more winning shots. You can observe the same in any sport. And you can certainly observe the same dynamic on your team.

Keeping score brings out our best because we inherently like to win. You must keep score to know whether you are winning, or you can easily end up with your team being very active but not very productive. You can keep score on your revenue, profitability, customer satisfaction, quality, prospect pipeline, cost per sales, employee engagement, defects, inventory, call-center response time and so on. There certainly is no lack of things to measure. To keep it simple, measure only what matters most. Do not measure everything. You can use the 80/20 principle here. Which 20 percent of the measures tell you 80 percent of the story? Those are the measures you want to track. Of course, if you are going to keep score, you need a scoreboard. You will want to design a scoreboard that is simple and clear, resonates with your team and is easy to update.

It's also a chance to be creative and visual with your team. Your scoreboard doesn't have to be a lackluster summary of your monthly business report showing key measures. Use your scoreboard to tell a clear and compelling story in as few words and numbers as possible. Consider some of these scoreboard formats:

- Visual thermometer with a rising mercury line to show progress.

- Traffic light (red, yellow and green indicators to show if you are off-plan, slightly off-plan or on-plan, respectively).

- A jar of jellybeans to illustrate percentage of completion.

- Emoticons ☺ ☹ or visual indicators such as thumbs up/thumbs down next to each goal. These emoticons work great for movie reviews and Facebook, so why not use them to help your team quickly see the score?

- A picture of an actual scoreboard to keep track of number of calls made, new customers, shipments, invoices processed, response time, customer complaints, new hires or whichever metrics are most important to your team.

Keeping your scoreboard updated is critical. Your scoreboard must be current to be compelling and be seen as a reliable reflection of performance. Understanding what is happening on your team empowers you to adjust continually, enhance accountability and boost results.

Excellent leaders get creative with scoreboards while keeping them relevant to the employees they are managing. For example, Stephen Mansfield, CEO of Methodist Health System in Dallas, has a handy technique to keep his team focused and reliable. His scorecard is literally just that – an index card. Mansfield says, "I have a little handwritten index card for each direct report. On that card, I write the three primary things that person and I have agreed that I most need from them. I check in with each person every few weeks to ask how they are doing on those items. I always end the discussion with, 'Is there anything I can do to help?'"[1] Mansfield is a master at creating the reliability advantage by measuring progress and results. Notice in his quote that he is also asking his team what he can do. This is a good example of how excellent leaders integrate the five coaching habits into their daily interactions.

Measure Results and Behavior

Measurement in and of itself is necessary but not sufficient. When someone performs well or poorly, your job is to involve the employee (Habit #3) in finding out why so he/she can either double down on the causes of good performance or change the causes of poor performance. Most leaders tend to focus their critique, feedback and training on symptoms rather than the root cause of poor performance. It ends up wasting time and resources. If you directly address the root cause, you will see immediate results. The fastest way to identify the cause is to closely observe performance, the work system and ask questions (Habit #2).

To get a more complete picture of performance, measure your team members' results and behavior. Achieving the performance standard on one of them is necessary but not sufficient to be a reliable performer. Getting results is great, but they will not be sustainable without the right behaviors. Wrong behaviors include being a poor teammate by not sharing information and resources, acting inconsistently with team and organizational values or disregarding agreed-to job processes (e.g., conducting quality checks, making "X" number of calls, using prescribed materials). Any of these behaviors put at risk the reliability of your team's results. On the other hand, acceptable behaviors do not necessarily guarantee results, so measuring both is key to continually improving your team's reliability.

You get the behaviors you are willing to tolerate. If you rank your team by performance level, your lowest performer is a public statement of the performance level you are willing to tolerate. That is what your team sees as your performance standard. Ignoring issues puts your team and your leadership credibility at risk. A small molehill-sized issue today that takes five minutes to proactively address can quickly expand into a mountain-sized matter that requires five days or more to resolve. Unaddressed performance matters do not just go away; instead, they eventually rear their heads in uglier ways.

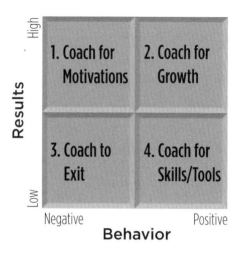

In the 2 x 2 matrix, you can see how the four combinations of measuring results and behaviors affect your coaching approach.

Quadrant 1 is the employee whose behavior is up to standard, but the results are not. These are the trickiest coaching situations because the employee is delivering results but his/her behavior is creating risk for the team. Focus on their behavioral motivations and be clear that you have an "and/both" not an "either/or" expectation; results and behaviors must meet standard. This is where some leaders put their integrity at risk – by tolerating the bull in the china shop because he delivers results, even though it might put the team and future reliability at risk.

Quadrant 2 employees are your stars, delivering results and doing it the right way. Encourage and look for opportunities to expand this employee's responsibilities and influence.

Quadrant 3 employees are not well suited for the role; so after appropriate coaching and support with no improvement on either performance dimension, don't waste time moving them out. Make your personnel decisions with rationality, but implement them with humanity.

Coach Quadrant 4 employees on the skills and tools needed to deliver results. They are likely willing to learn since they are already meeting your behavior standards. That said, be clear and specific with your language and improvement expectations. Keep it simple with the 3W format that we discussed in the Explain chapter – What needs to improve, who is responsible and by when?

There's a phrase – *The main thing is to keep the main thing the main thing.* When employees understand what the main thing is and have a clear concept of what is required of them, measurements can become their friends. Measurements are encouraging and validating to high-performing employees and provide an objective case to improve for lower-performing employees.

The **5** Coaching Habits

1 EXPLAIN
Expectations ➤ **Alignment**

2 ASK
Questions ➤ **Engagement**

3 INVOLVE
Team ➤ **Ownership**

4 MEASURE
Results ➤ **Accountability**

- Measure what matters most.

- Use relevant scoreboards.

- Measure results and behavior.

★

Measuring results is the first step
toward improving them.

★

★ Taking Action ★

MEASURE
Results ➟ Accountability

1. What are one or two key measures of success for each of my team members?

2. What is the simplest, real-time method to keep score for your key measures of success?

 What gets measured gets done, so measure what matters most.

Coaching Habit #5

APPRECIATE
People ➡ **Commitment**

Everyone has an invisible sign
hanging from their neck saying,
'Make me feel important.'
Never forget this message when working with people.

— Mary Kay Ash,
founder of Mary Kay Cosmetics

William James, the father of psychology, stated that the most fundamental psychological need is to be appreciated. We want to feel fully appreciated for our work. Unfortunately, the reality is that lack of appreciation is the No. 1 reason people leave their jobs. The direct supervisor is the primary source of appreciation (or lack thereof), the primary influencer of job satisfaction and engagement, and a primary reason people either leave or stay on the job.

Demonstrating appreciation is not a matter of time and intention; it is a matter of priority and action. That said, showing appreciation is a common blind spot for leaders – and for people in any relationship, for that matter. You no doubt feel appreciative of your team; yet predictably there is a gap between how much your team feels appreciated and how much you feel that you appreciate them. Why is that? This disconnect exists because you likely don't convert every thought of appreciation into visible acts of appreciation. While we judge ourselves by our intentions, others judge us by our actions. What is important is not how much you appreciate people, but rather how much you *demonstrate* that appreciation.

A survey of 15 million people worldwide illuminates the business benefits of appreciation. This Gallup study by Tom Rath and Donald Clifton found that people who receive regular recognition at work:

- Experience increased productivity;

- Enjoy increased engagement with colleagues;

- Are more likely to stay with the organization;

- Receive higher loyalty and satisfaction scores from customers;

- Have better safety records and fewer accidents on the job.[1]

Appreciation comes down to basic psychology: Reinforce those behaviors that you want to see more frequently. Look for opportunities to recognize and appreciate your team's efforts and results. Catch them doing something right … and do it often.

Look for Yellow Cars

We have a special family tradition with our children. For their 12th birthday, they can select any city in the continental United States to visit for a special celebration with just Mom and Dad – no siblings. Our middle child, Grace, decided on New York to celebrate her 12th birthday. Having been there many times ourselves, it was fun to see the wonderment in a first-time visitor's eyes as she took in the lights of Times Square, the windows of the shops along 5th Avenue, the view from the Empire State Building and the ethnic richness of Chinatown and Little Italy.

Since our hotel was near Times Square, we walked a well-worn path down Broadway during our stay. Times Square really is the ultimate in sensory overload. During nearly a dozen trips down the same street, we noticed something new every time. Whatever item we were looking for seemed to magically appear even though we had previously walked past it numerous times without noticing – a souvenir shop, a deli, a street vendor selling scarves, a hot dog stand, live musicians or Italian cannolis. Whatever we were looking for seemed to pop out from the array of visual stimuli of

Times Square. This experience reminded us once again that when you change the way you look at things, things change the way they look.

The things we pay the most attention to reflect what we think about most. The reverse is also true. If we change what we think about, what we notice in our surroundings will change. For example, when was the last time you saw a yellow car that wasn't a taxi? Maybe last week or last month? Now that we have made you aware of yellow cars and you are thinking about them, you will start seeing more of them. Is there going to be a sudden invasion of bright yellow cars? Of course not; they've been there all along. The difference is, in the days ahead, you will be thinking about them and, therefore, more readily notice yellow cars.

We call this connection between our thoughts and our attention "The Yellow Car Phenomenon." This phenomenon is rooted in neuroscience. The Reticular Activating System (RAS) is the mechanism in the human brain that brings relevant information to your attention.[2] In essence, the RAS is the brain's filter between the subconscious and conscious mind. Without you being aware of it, the RAS sifts through the millions of pieces of information, stimuli and data coming into your brain from all your senses. It then filters out the irrelevant and brings only the relevant information to your conscious mind.

So, the RAS decides what you put your attention toward. It allows your conscious mind to focus only on that which you've determined is useful right now. This explains why, on our walks down Broadway in New York City, we didn't notice the Italian cannolis when we were looking for scarves and vice versa, but once we were hungry, we saw cannolis galore! And it's why you'll start seeing yellow cars now that we've planted the information in your RAS that yellow cars are relevant.

You can leverage "The Yellow Car Phenomenon" to help you demonstrate appreciation for your team, and as a result, deepen their commitment. Simply make good performance your Yellow Car. Look for things they are doing well and reinforce it. For example, recognize positive movement or effort toward the goal. Demonstrate your appreciation for their *approach*, not just their results, such as:

- Presenting a professional image,

- Always looking for a win-win,

- Encouraging team members,

- Staying focused at work when they have lots of distractions at home,

- Consistently meeting deadlines or presenting top-quality work.

If you make positive efforts and results your "Yellow Car," you will find plenty of positive performances to appreciate and, therefore, deepen your team's commitment.

Sincere and Specific

After interviewing 25,000 leaders, Ferdinand Fournies found the most effective leaders had one thing in common – they expressed a sincere interest in their employees.[3] "Sincere" is the operative word here. Your motivation matters! If you appreciate employees in hopes of getting something in return, they will see right through you.

You have complete control over your appreciation. No budget limitations or excuses here. There are literally thousands of ways to demonstrate your appreciation at little or no cost. You can occasionally offer a gift card or something of modest value, but you should rely more on your creativity and knowledge of the employee to personalize your appreciation so it is meaningful. The key to appreciation is making it sincere and specific. Don't fall into the trap of blurting out the robotic, "Good job." Take the time to explain *why* you appreciate an employee's performance, such as, "I really appreciate the way you kept our customer happy without incurring more cost."

In our work at client organizations, we have seen more than a few handwritten notes of appreciation on employees' desks. Often these cards are several years old (up to five years in one case), yet still prominently and proudly displayed. We often wonder if the leaders who wrote them understand how much discretionary effort their three-minute investment yielded or know how meaningful those cards were to those employees. Daniel Jones is Chairman, President and CEO of Encore Wire, a publicly traded leader in the copper wire industry for over 25 years. He says, "Even as the world has become more high-tech, I have continued to send employees handwritten notes of appreciation. Based on the feedback, I am convinced that the personal touch has even greater impact with today's worker."[4] Jones' testimony reinforces that we work in a high-tech world, but leadership is still a high-touch job.

Find a way to express your appreciation that is natural to you. Not everyone is a notecard writer, but every leader has a way of showing appreciation that feels authentic. As long as your appreciation is specific and sincere, you don't need to worry about going overboard. In fact, there are no documented studies of employees ever feeling over-appreciated! The sky is the limit.

Know the Person Behind the Employee

To ignite commitment, appreciate not only good performance, but also appreciate the person. It is easy to appreciate the top performers who bail you out of tight spots or whose hard work makes you look good. It is more challenging, but more meaningful, to appreciate the person. You can appreciate reliability on the job, service to others outside of work, consistently professional demeanor or attire, integrity in gray situations, willingness to coach new team members, optimistic outlook, or ability to keep personal challenges at home and remain focused on the job.

Appreciation is certainly not a one-size-fits-all need. It should be customized to each employee, so personalize your recognition. For example, being recognized at an all-employee meeting might trigger more perspiration than inspiration for an introverted employee. Instead, use the information you learn about your employees to present an appropriate gift, token or sincere expression of appreciation. Your gesture will be less important than the obvious time and thoughtfulness that went into it.

Learn something new each day about one of your employees. Keep a file at your desk, on your computer or even on your phone with a few key notes about each team member's hobbies, favorite things and family. Then weave this information into your interactions with them and recognition for them. They will return your appreciation with deeper personal commitment and discretionary effort. Know your people, not just your employees. You will begin to understand them more fully and be able to more effectively express your appreciation … and deepen their commitment.

What's Your Ratio?

Research by the former chairman of Gallup, the late Donald Clifton, revealed that workgroups with at least a 3-to-1 ratio of positive-to-negative interactions were significantly more productive than those having less than a 3-to-1 ratio. The same study showed the key ratio for marriages was 5-to-1.[5] What is the ratio for your team? Is it 1:1, 3:1, 5:1 or 10:1? Here are a few easy ways to boost your team's ratio:

- Say "Thank You!" – an all-too-obvious yet highly underused form of appreciation.

- Allow employees to present their work to your boss. This is a great way to engage employees, and it also shows *your* boss what kind of leader you are.

- Offer team members a choice of projects to work on. When employees buy into a project, they will put their hearts into it.

- Put a sincere acknowledgement in your company or department newsletter. This takes only a few minutes of your time, but creates long-term "trophy value" for the employee.

- Tell an employee's story of accomplishment at a staff meeting. Stories are perceived as more interesting, meaningful, thoughtful and memorable.

- Take a team member to lunch to show your appreciation. Remember to do more listening than talking.

Consider tracking your team's ratio for a week to gauge how well you are appreciating your employees. Don't worry about showing too much appreciation. And remember, there are no documented cases of employees, or anyone else for that matter, feeling *over*-appreciated!

Do you remember a time you received a card or note of thanks from your boss? Did you throw it away? Probably not. Employee appreciation goes a long way. In the midst of many other problems at work, employees will remain loyal and reliable if they feel like they are valued and recognized. Your ROIT (return on invested time) is higher than nearly any other investment you can make, resulting in a team that is committed to your goals and committed to you as a leader.

The 5 Coaching Habits

1 EXPLAIN
Expectations ➡ **Alignment**

2 ASK
Questions ➡ **Engagement**

3 INVOLVE
Team ➡ Ownership

4 MEASURE
Results ➡ Accountability

5 APPRECIATE
People ➡ **Commitment**

- Make positive performance your "Yellow Car."

- Know the person behind the employee.

- Boost your ratio of positive/negative interactions.

★

People do more for those who appreciate them.

★

★ Taking Action ★

APPRECIATE
People ➡ **Commitment**

1. What one thought of appreciation can I convert into an act of appreciation today?

2. What personal reminder system can I use to ensure I appreciate my team at least once a day?

 Appreciation is not a matter of time and intention;
rather, it is a matter of priority and action.

Personal Reliability

x

Coaching Reliability

=

The 5 Coaching Habits of Excellent Leaders
At-a-Glance

Coaching Habits	Results	Leadership Actions
1 **EXPLAIN** Expectations	Alignment	• Answer the fundamental four questions (goals, plans, roles and rewards). • Align on the 3W's – What, Who and When. • Coach up your team by moving down the learning pyramid.
2 **ASK** Questions	Engagement	• Define your objective before you ask. • Get comfortable with silence after you ask. • After you ask, listen to eliminate blind spots.
3 **INVOLVE** Team	Ownership	• Seek those with under-the-hood knowledge. • Involve to improve. • Define team involvement roles.
4 **MEASURE** Results	Accountability	• Measure what matters most. • Use relevant scoreboards. • Measure results and behavior.
5 **APPRECIATE** People	Commitment	• Make positive performance your "Yellow Car." • Know the person behind the employee. • Boost your ratio of positive/negative interactions.

Take a free, three-minute self-assessment of your personal and team reliability at: www.theLgroup.com/coaching

Winning Habits

Successful people are simply those with successful habits.

— BRIAN TRACY,
author, *The Psychology of Achievement*

The poem titled, *"Who am I?"* by an unknown author, serves as a poignant introduction to this chapter:

I am your constant companion.

I am your greatest helper or heaviest burden.

I will push you onward or drag you down to failure.

I am completely at your command.

Half the things you do you might just as well turn over to me, and I will be able to do them quickly, correctly.

I am easily managed – you must merely be firm with me. Show me exactly how you want something done, and after a few lessons I will do it automatically.

I am the servant of all great people; and alas, of all failures as well. Those who are failures, I have made failures.

I am not a machine, though I work with all the precision of a machine plus the intelligence of a human being.

You may run me for a profit or turn me for ruin – it makes no difference to me.

Take me, train me, be firm with me, and I will place the world at your feet.

Be easy with me and I will destroy you.

Who am I?

I am habit.

Nearly half of your daily activities are habitual, for better or for worse. You don't think about them, you just do them. You have simple habits like walking where those with healthy legs do not think about putting one foot in front of the other. You also have more complex habits like driving where you likely recall a time when you pulled into your driveway after a long day at work and thought, "Oh my! How in the world did I get here?" There are also modern habits like waking up and instinctively grabbing your phone to check your email. So how do you take charge of your habits?

Start Small

The key to finishing big is to start small. Big achievements like running a marathon, introducing a new product or exceeding a hefty sales goal all start with one small step. Consistent "baby steps" lead to BIG places. The same holds true when you are embracing new habits to boost your personal and team reliability.

An important first step is to know yourself. The greatest kind of knowledge is self-knowledge. Your strengths can't benefit you if you don't know how to leverage them. By the same token, your greatest liability is the one you are unaware of.

So, stop right now and take a moment to complete this three-minute, online self-assessment: www.theLgroup.com/coaching.

Your real-time feedback report will help you immediately in two ways. First, the assessment will identify your baseline, your starting point, by measuring your current level of personal and team reliability. Second, it will identify initial steps you can take to boost your performance. Start with one small step today to have a big impact tomorrow.

Your Triggers

At work, the daily whirlwind demands of the job and your team can easily push you back into poor habits, such as being reactive (vs. proactive) and can also force you to abandon what you know to be positive leadership habits like the five coaching habits. So, reflect on specific triggers that may prevent you from sticking to the five coaching habits. For example, whenever you feel stressed, you tend to tell your team what to do instead of ask for their input. Another trigger could be when meetings run long you start to feel rushed, so you do not wrap up with the 3W's (What, Who and When) to ensure the team is aligned on expectations. Maybe there are times when your team is doing well and things are going smoothly, maybe even too smoothly for you to feel comfortable, so you find something trivial the team could improve instead of appreciating its performance.

Write down your triggers and look at them relative to your self-assessment results. See if there is a connection between the areas where you scored lowest and your triggers. Next, write a specific action you will take to neutralize your triggers so you can consistently apply the five coaching habits.

Commit to Your Team, Not Yourself

We tend to view a commitment to others as deeper and stronger than a commitment to ourselves, in part because it creates more public accountability. Reflect on why maintaining the five coaching habits is important to your team members, personally and professionally. Remember that excellent leadership is about others, not ourselves. Every time you apply one of the coaching habits, you are enhancing a team member's life and work with a nice ripple effect into your business and customers.

Every time you choose to say "yes" to some other activity and forgo one of the coaching habits, you are robbing that same team member. He/she has lost an opportunity to grow, contribute and succeed, and all the beneficiaries of that growth, contribution and success are then robbed of the positive impact he/she might have otherwise received. You are the leadership pebble in the lake of many people's lives. So, find your own compelling purpose for making the five coaching habits part of your daily leadership, then be bold enough to share it with your team.

Your B.E.S.T. Team

The strength of our relationships is perhaps the greatest measure of the quality of our lives. It is also a key predictor of our team's performance. We should act our best and give our best to our relationships. They are built on two-way streets and must be mutually beneficial; each person must bring something of value. Otherwise, our relationships will not endure, and our team's performance will not be sustainable.

Friends pull you up. Friends encourage you in your pursuit of wisdom by offering their own. Take some time to think of people who have made a difference for you and for whom you have made a difference. The is your B.E.S.T. team: Buddies who Encourage Success and Truth.

Choose wisely those you want on your team. Ensure they offer the energy, truth and positive perspective you need to orchestrate your actions. There is no better test than time when it comes to relationships, so start small and build your B.E.S.T. team slowly. The key is to connect with your B.E.S.T. team, individually, or as a group, on a consistent basis.

Depending on the relationship, we can play the role of teacher and/or student. In either role, we all need people who will support our success. Your B.E.S.T. team can help you:

- Hone your self-awareness. Depend on your B.E.S.T. team to give you truthful, constructive feedback.

- Provide a chance to help them. As the Proverb says, "In teaching others, we teach ourselves."

- Provide support to combat resistance you might receive from implementing your new coaching habits.

- Rehearse challenging situations before you have a live performance.

Your B.E.S.T. team is a personal and powerful way to ensure you are being reliable and inspiring reliable team performance.

Good Student – Great Coach

Your team looks to you as its role model for leading and learning. What does it see? Does it look like you know it all, like you are stuck in the past or like you are just cruising? The key to being a great coach is being a good student. It all starts with you! If your team sees your thirst for and openness to learning, they will model the same behavior. It's certainly nice to be comfortable in your role, but growth and learning typically occur when you are uncomfortable.

Excellent leadership is not just about investing in others. It's also about investing in yourself. Today more than ever, there is a virtual olympics of learning activities and opportunities available to you. The great news is that to elevate your performance there is no annual membership fee to the brain gym! All we need to exercise our brains is at our fingertips, literally. But it's not just about reading and training.

The brain gym is anywhere you want it to be. In other words, your life is your own learning lab, where you can build your leadership competence. You can find best practices everywhere. Watch the people around you. You can find nuggets of excellence from a father-in-law, a clergyman, a speaker at a professional association meeting, a fellow leader, your child's school principal, a Boy Scout's troop leader or a particularly helpful salesperson at a local department store. Observe, read, ask, listen and learn.

There are also lessons to be learned in everything your team does. Look for learning opportunities in post-project reviews, customer meetings, conflicts with other departments, changes in priorities, miscommunications and mistakes. Seize all these experiences to exercise your brain. Keeping your membership at the brain gym continually hones your competence … and competence builds confidence. Confidence is critical; excellent leaders need it, and their teams want to see it. If you want to be a great coach, be a good student.

The Reliability Advantage

Creating the reliability advantage for your team is a leadership marathon that is won with daily sprints. If you maintain your daily coaching habits, then victory is yours. You will predictably create the reliability advantage and reap all the benefits it brings, personally and professionally. You have already taken the first step by reading this book. What's your next step?

---★---

You don't have to be great to start,
but you have to start to be great.

– ZIG ZIGLAR,
author and motivational speaker

---★---

Reinforcement Resources

1. **Executive Coaching**
   The Executive Navigation^{SM} coaching process is results-focused and supported by field-tested tools to help you elevate your leadership. Clients measurably improve personal productivity, team reliability and performance.

2. **Keynote Presentation**
   Invite the authors to present a high-energy, engaging look at how excellent leaders inspire reliable performance by using *The 5 Coaching Habits* and how you can apply the same principles.

3. **Workshop**
   Delivered by one of the authors or a certified facilitator, this half- or full-day interactive workshop delivers simple tools that participants can put to work right away to boost their personal and team reliability.

4. **Accountability Video and Team Discussion Series**
   The Specifics of Accountability is a just-add-water video and team discussion series to help leaders boost their team's accountability. Each of three modules contains a short video, actionable tools and team discussion for specific expectations, coaching and language. These short, 15-minute modules are designed to be integrated into existing team meetings for maximum efficiency and impact.

5. **Leaders' PowerPoint® Briefing Presentation**
   Introduce *The 5 Coaching Habits of Excellent Leaders* to your team or entire organization. This detailed and professionally designed presentation equips you to confidently and competently present all the key points and insights from the book. Use the presentation for staff meetings, workshops or brown bag lunches.

6. **Complimentary Self-Assessment**
   The best knowledge is self-knowledge. This three-minute, complimentary, online assessment delivers a real-time feedback report. Assess your personal and team reliability at: www.theLgroup.com/coaching

7. **Complimentary Leadership Tips and Tools**
   Receive our short weekly posts directly to your inbox: Just text "Leadership" to 444-999 for free weekly tips to elevate your leadership today!

To learn more:

theLgroup.com
972-250-9989

About the Authors

Lee J. Colan, Ph.D. is a high-energy leadership advisor, engaging speaker and popular author. He was nominated for the *Thinkers50* Award for best management thinker globally. Lee has authored 14 popular leadership books, including two best-sellers that have been translated into 10 languages. His cut-through-the-clutter advice is anchored in his corporate leadership experience and robust consulting business.

Lee earned his doctorate in Industrial/Organizational Psychology from George Washington University after graduating from Florida State University.

Julie Davis-Colan is an innovative business advisor and peak performance coach with experience in sales and marketing to *Fortune 500* companies. Julie has authored six popular books. She has been coaching and encouraging positive behavior change for 30 years while focusing on organizational health and peak performance. Additionally, Julie is a compelling speaker and engaging trainer. Her passion for leadership and life creates an infectious energy for audiences.

Julie earned her Master's degree in Preventive Medicine from The Ohio State University, College of Medicine, after graduating from Florida State University.

THE **L** GROUP

Leadership at every level.

Consulting: Our top-notch consultants deliver cut-through-the-clutter insights that drive results for your team.

Executive Coaching: Our advisors help executives boost team and personal performance.

Speaking: Engage your team with passionate delivery and equip them with practical tools.

Resources: Rapid-read books, multimedia training tools and leadership assessments.

Training: Rely on our certified facilitators (English- or Spanish-speaking) or use our just-add-water training kits for internal delivery.

theLgroup.com   972.250.9989

Notes

Personal Reliability

1. Notes from author Steve Williford during interview with Ken May, 2001
2. http://www.astronomycafe.net/qadir/q1835.html
3. Paul Spiegelman, personal interview, June 12, 2012

Coaching Reliability

1. Jeanne Bliss, Chief Customer Officer 2.0: How to Build Your Customer-Driven Growth Engine (New York, Jossey-Bass, 2006)
2. Elaine Agather, personal interview, July 12, 2012

Habit #1: EXPLAIN Expectations

1. Peter Gollwitzer, "Goal Achievement: The Role of Intentions," European Review of Social Psychology, vol. 4 (Hoboken, NJ: John Wiley & Sons Ltd, 1993)

Habit #2: ASK Questions

1. *Seinfeld, Little Kicks* episode 138, written by Spike Feresten, directed by Andy Ackerman, aired Oct. 10, 1996. Script archived at: http://www.seinfeldscripts.com/TheLittleKicks.htm
2. Ibid.
3. Andrew Levi, personal interview, July 3, 2012

Habit #3: INVOLVE Team

1. Bob Bunker, personal interview, Oct. 17, 2012

Habit #4: MEASURE Results

1. Stephen Mansfield, personal interview, June 14, 2012

Habit #5: APPRECIATE People

1. Tom Rath and Donald O. Clifton. *How Full Is Your Bucket?* (New York: Gallup, 2004)
2. Alvin Silverstein and Virginia Silverstein, *World of the Brain* (New York: William Morrow, 1986)
3. Ferdinand F. Fournies, *Why Employees Don't Do What They're Supposed to Do and What to Do About It* (New York: McGraw-Hill, 1999)
4. Daniel Jones, personal interview, Jan. 27, 2017.
5. Tom Rath and Donald O. Clifton. *How Full Is Your Bucket?* (New York: Gallup, 2004)

The 5 Coaching Habits of Excellent Leaders
Package

Includes all books pictured for

Only $79!

($108 value)

For additional leadership resources, visit
theLgroup.com

☑ **YES! Please send me extra copies of**
The 5 Coaching Habits of Excellent Leaders!

1-30 copies $16.95   31-100 copies $15.95   101+ copies $14.95

The 5 Coaching Habits of Excellent Leaders	____ copies X	_____	= $ _____
The 5 Coaching Habits Powerpoint™	____ copies X $99.95		= $ _____
The 5 Coaching Habits package	____ copies X $79.00		= $ _____

Other books by the authors:

Sticking to It: The Art of Adherence	____ copies X $10.95	= $ _____
Passionate Performance	____ copies X $10.95	= $ _____
Orchestrating Attitude	____ copies X $10.95	= $ _____
107 Ways to Stick to It	____ copies X $10.95	= $ _____
7 Moments…That Define Excellent Leaders	____ copies X $14.95	= $ _____
Leadership Matters	____ copies X $16.95	= $ _____
The Nature of Excellence (Classic Edition)	____ copies X $15.95	= $ _____

Shipping & Handling $ _____

Subtotal $ _____

Sales Tax (8.25%-TX Only) $ _____

Total (U.S. Dollars Only) $ _____

Shipping and Handling Charges

tal $ Amount	Up to $49	$50-$99	$100-$249	$250-$1199	$1200-$2999	$3000+
harge	$7	$9	$16	$30	$80	$125

Name _____   Job Title _____

Organization _____   Phone _____

Shipping Address _____   Fax _____

Billing Address _____ Email _____
(Required for downloadable products)

City _____ State _____ ZIP _____

☐ Please invoice (Orders over $200) Purchase Order Number (if applicable) _____

Charge Your Order: ☐ MasterCard   ☐ Visa   ☐ American Express

Credit Card Number _____ Exp. Date _____

Signature _____

☐ Check Enclosed (Payable to: CornerStone Leadership)

Mail: P.O. Box 764087
Dallas, TX 75376

Fax: 972.274.2884   Phone: 972.298.8377

Thank you for reading
The 5 Coaching Habits of Excellent Leaders.

CornerStone Leadership Institute
is committed to providing practical resources
to organizations worldwide.

CornerStone
Leadership Institute

www.CornerStoneLeadership.com

Start a crusade in your organization.
Have the courage to learn, the vision to lead
and the passion to share.